HELEN KELLER AND ALEXANDER GRAHAM BELL

By Jill Keppeler

Gareth Stevens
PUBLISHING

Please visit our website, www.garethstevens.com. For a free color catalog of all our high-quality books, call toll free 1-800-542-2595 or fax 1-877-542-2596.

Library of Congress Cataloging-in-Publication Data

Names: Keppeler, Jill, author.
Title: Helen Keller and Alexander Graham Bell / Jill Keppeler.
Description: New York : Gareth Stevens Publishing, [2022] | Series: History's famous friendships | Includes bibliographical references and index.
Identifiers: LCCN 2020040174 (print) | LCCN 2020040175 (ebook) | ISBN 9781538264959 (library binding) | ISBN 9781538264935 (paperback) | ISBN 9781538264942 (set) | ISBN 9781538264966 (ebook)
Subjects: LCSH: Keller, Helen, 1880-1968--Friends and associates--Juvenile literature. | Bell, Alexander Graham, 1847-1922--Friends and associates--Juvenile literature. | Deafblind women--United States--Biography--Juvenile literature.
Classification: LCC HV1624.K4 K47 2022 (print) | LCC HV1624.K4 (ebook) | DDC 362.4/1092273--dc23
LC record available at https://lccn.loc.gov/2020040174
LC ebook record available at https://lccn.loc.gov/2020040175

First Edition

Published in 2022 by
Gareth Stevens Publishing
111 East 14th Street, Suite 349
New York, NY 10003

Copyright © 2022 Gareth Stevens Publishing

Designer: Katelyn E. Reynolds
Editor: Therese Shea

Photo credits: Cvr, pp. 1 (both), 7, 11, 15, 18, 20, 21, 23, 29 (Bell) courtesy of the Library of Congress; cvr, pp. 1-32 (background) wawritto/Shutterstock.com; pp. 1-32 (frame) Olesia Misty/Shutterstock.com; cvr, pp. 1-32 (border) Vasya Kobelev/Shutterstock.com; p. 5 PhotoQuest/Getty Images; p. 6 SSPL/Getty Images; pp. 9, 12, 13, 16 Bettmann/Getty Images; p. 10 laurien/E+/Getty Images; p. 15 (inset) Bengt Geijerstam/Photolibrary/Getty Images Plus; pp. 17, 19 Chicago History Museum/Getty Images; p. 22 © CORBIS/Corbis via Getty Images; p. 25 Joe Sohm/Visions of America/Universal Images Group via Getty Images; p. 26 Evans/Three Lions/Getty Images; p. 27 Topical Press Agency/Getty Images; p. 29 (Keller) Oscar White/Corbis/VCG via Getty Images.

CPSIA compliance information: Batch #CSGS22: For further information contact Gareth Stevens, New York, New York at 1-800-542-2595.

Find us on

CONTENTS

Words in the Glossary appear in **bold** type the first time they are used in the text.

TWO VERY DIFFERENT PEOPLE

When they met, one was a 6-year-old American girl. The other was a Scottish-born man who was nearly 40. She was blind and **deaf.** She needed a better way to learn and connect with the world. He was a teacher and scientist who had invented the telephone.

These two people—Helen Keller and Alexander Graham Bell—would go on to make a big difference in each other's lives. They would change people's views about those with **disabilities** and become lifelong friends.

This photo shows Helen Keller and Alexander Graham Bell in 1901, when Keller was 21 and Bell was 54.

5

TEACHER AND INVENTOR

Alexander Graham Bell was born in 1847 in Scotland. His family later moved to England and then Canada. Finally, Bell settled in the United States. He began teaching at schools for deaf students, starting in Boston, Massachusetts.

Bell was also an inventor. He worked on improving the **telegraph**. He invented the telephone in 1876. He would later improve the phonograph, or record player, which was originally created by Thomas Edison. Bell also worked on other inventions, including airplanes and boats.

early telephone by Alexander Graham Bell

Alexander Graham Bell was about 14 years old when this photo was taken.

MORE TO KNOW

BELL'S FATHER TAUGHT DEAF STUDENTS, AND HIS MOTHER WAS ALMOST DEAF. THIS HAD AN EFFECT ON HIS JOB CHOICES.

A GIRL WHO WANTED TO LEARN

Helen Keller wasn't always deaf and blind. When she was born in 1880, she could hear and see. However, she became very ill when she was 19 months old. She lost both senses.

When she was about 6, Keller's parents traveled to Baltimore, Maryland, to meet a doctor. This man had helped others with eye problems. However, he told them he couldn't help Keller. He sent them to someone who might be able to help her learn—Alexander Graham Bell.

MORE TO KNOW

KELLER CREATED HER OWN BASIC FORM OF SIGN LANGUAGE AS A CHILD. HOWEVER, SHE STILL COULDN'T **COMMUNICATE** WELL WITH OTHERS.

Keller was 7 years old in this photo. She was born in Tuscumbia, Alabama.

FIRST MEETING

In 1886, Alexander Graham Bell was already a famous inventor. At the time, he was working with deaf children in Washington, DC. He agreed to meet with Keller and her parents.

Keller remembered that first meeting well. She later wrote about it in her **autobiography**, *The Story of My Life*. Bell caused his pocket watch to make a noise so she could feel its **vibrations**. She said he understood her signs, "and I knew it and loved him at once."

pocket watch

This photo shows Bell, his wife Mabel, and his daughters
Elsie (left) and Marian in 1885, a year before he met Helen Keller.

CONNECTIONS

What Alexander Graham Bell did next changed Helen Keller's life forever. He told her father to write to the Perkins Institution for the Blind to ask for a teacher for his daughter. Keller's father did.

That teacher, Anne Sullivan, arrived in March 1887. Teaching Keller wasn't easy at first. However, Sullivan finally started getting through to her. The little girl began to learn words and signs quickly. Sullivan wrote to Bell, calling it a **miracle.** Bell spread the news of Keller and Sullivan's success.

Helen Keller

This photo of Helen Keller and Anne Sullivan was taken in 1893. Keller called the day she met Sullivan "my soul's birthday."

13

LEARNING AND TRAVELING

Helen Keller continued to learn words and signs. She went to school to learn Braille. This is a system of writing for the blind that uses characters made up of raised dots. Keller also started learning to speak **verbally**. When she was 14, she went to school in New York City.

During this time, Keller stayed in touch with Bell. She and Anne Sullivan traveled to meet him again when Keller was about 8. They also met President Grover Cleveland, the first of many presidents Keller would meet.

MORE TO KNOW

KELLER MET EVERY U.S. PRESIDENT FROM GROVER CLEVELAND TO LYNDON B. JOHNSON. THAT'S 13 PRESIDENTS!

Braille

Twelve-year-old Helen Keller was there when building began for Bell's Volta Bureau, a library for the deaf in Washington, DC.

15

THE WORLD'S FAIR

Helen Keller and Anne Sullivan went with Alexander Graham Bell to the World's Columbian Exposition in 1893. It was held in Chicago, Illinois. Bell acted as Keller's guide. He taught her about the **exhibits** they found there. The president of the fair told Keller she could touch the fair's exhibits. She learned about mining diamonds, stood on model ships, and found out more about other places. Later, in her autobiography, Keller wrote, "Every day in imagination I made a trip around the world."

Helen Keller

Anne Sullivan

Visitors look out over the site of the 1893 World's Columbian Exposition in Chicago. It was also called the World's Fair.

Bell, Sullivan, and Keller visited the World's Fair for three weeks. Keller wrote about how Bell explained telephones, phonographs, and other inventions to her. He also showed her items from history, including tools from ancient Mexico and Egyptian mummies. She chose not to touch the mummies!

After the visit, Keller wrote a letter to Mabel Bell, Alexander Graham Bell's wife. "In the years that are to come," she wrote, "I shall derive [take] more and more enjoyment from my pleasant recollections [memories] of the Fair."

Alexander Graham Bell

Mabel Bell

Keller really enjoyed the area at the fair called the Midway Plaisance. It included a Ferris wheel, which she got to ride.

HEADING TO COLLEGE

As she grew older, Helen Keller wanted to attend college. Alexander Graham Bell supported her in this dream. In 1896, he started a **trust fund** for her. Keller started attending the Cambridge School for Young Ladies in Massachusetts. Later, she took tests for Radcliffe College, which is now part of Harvard University, and passed.

In 1900, when she was about 20, Keller started at Radcliffe. The trust fund and more money from Bell paid for this education.

Where Helen Keller went, Anne Sullivan went. She helped Keller at both the Cambridge School and Radcliffe College. This photo shows them in 1896.

MORE TO KNOW

HELEN KELLER DIDN'T LIKE THE LACK OF FREE TIME SHE HAD IN COLLEGE. "ONE GOES TO COLLEGE TO LEARN, IT SEEMS, NOT TO THINK," SHE WROTE.

College was hard for both Keller and Sullivan. While Keller worked hard and studied, the two women had to do more than double the work Keller's classmates did. Sullivan listened to classes and repeated them to Keller through signs. She also read Keller's non-Braille books to her in this way.

However, all the hard work paid off. In 1904, Keller **graduated** with honors from Radcliffe College. Bell, who had never graduated from college, had helped her make her dream come true.

MORE TO KNOW

HELEN KELLER WAS THE FIRST DEAF AND BLIND PERSON TO ATTEND AND GRADUATE COLLEGE.

Helen Keller earned a bachelor of arts **degree** from Radcliffe. She changed many people's ideas about those with disabilities by doing this.

VISITING
CAPE BRETON

While Helen Keller had to study a lot in college, she also made time to do other things. She visited Bell often at his house on Cape Breton Island, Nova Scotia, Canada.

Keller wrote about a day when Bell made a boat that could be moved by a kite in the air. Keller could tell that wires connecting the dragon kite and boat weren't strong enough. She told Bell, but he sent up the kite anyway. The wires broke. After that, he asked Keller if the strings were OK first.

MORE TO KNOW

HELEN KELLER WROTE ABOUT THE KITE EVENT IN HER AUTOBIOGRAPHY: "THE WIRES BROKE, AND OFF WENT THE GREAT RED DRAGON, AND POOR DR. BELL STOOD LOOKING FORLORNLY [SADLY] AFTER IT."

This photo shows Bell's home in 2001. While Keller visited, she and Bell would talk about his work and her studies. Sometimes he did experiments and told her about them.

A DEDICATION

Alexander Graham Bell learned to use a Braille typewriter so he could write letters to Helen Keller. She also used a Braille typewriter. She used it to write her autobiography, *The Story of My Life*, which was released in 1903. She had worked on it while doing her classes in college.

Keller **dedicated** the book to Bell. She wrote, "To Alexander Graham Bell, who has taught the deaf to speak and enabled [allowed] the listening ear to hear speech from the Atlantic to the Rockies."

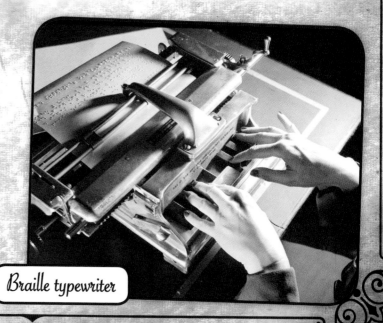

Braille typewriter

Helen Keller went on to write more books, including *The World I Live In*, which came out in 1908.

THE DAY THE PHONES WERE SILENT

Alexander Graham Bell died August 2, 1922. Helen Keller was 42 years old. They were friends until his death. On the day of Bell's **funeral**, every telephone in the United States was silent in his honor for one minute.

Keller lived to be 87 years old. She wrote and spoke around the world. She changed the way people everywhere thought of those with disabilities. Together, Bell and Keller made a huge difference in the world.

MORE TO KNOW

ANNE SULLIVAN LIVED TO BE 70 YEARS OLD, DYING IN 1936. SHE STAYED WITH KELLER UNTIL HER DEATH.

The Lives of Bell and Keller

1847
Alexander Graham Bell is born on March 3.

1871
Bell moves to the United States.

1876
Bell invents the telephone.

1880
Helen Keller is born on June 27.

1886
Keller's parents take her to meet Bell.

1887
Keller meets Anne Sullivan.

1896
Bell creates a trust fund for Keller. She enters the Cambridge School.

1900
Keller enters Radcliffe College.

1903
Keller publishes her autobiography, The Story of My Life.

1904
Keller graduates from Radcliffe with honors.

1922
Bell dies at age 75 on August 2.

1936
Anne Sullivan dies at age 70 on October 20.

1968
Helen Keller dies at age 87 on June 1.

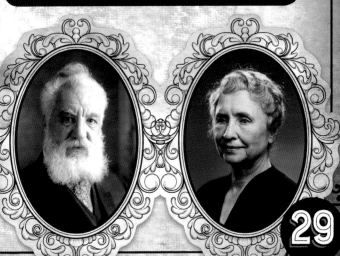

GLOSSARY

autobiography: a book written by someone about their life

communicate: to share ideas and feelings through sounds and motions

deaf: unable to hear

dedicate: to say that something was written or is being performed to honor someone

degree: a title given to someone who has completed a course of study at a college or university

disability: a condition that makes it hard for a person to do certain things

exhibit: something that's on display

funeral: a ceremony to mark the burial of the dead

graduate: to earn a degree or diploma from a school, college, or university

miracle: an amazing or unusual event

telegraph: a communication device that uses electric signals sent through wires

trust fund: money that belongs to one person but is legally held or managed by another person

verbally: having to do with words, spoken instead of written

vibration: a rapid movement back and forth

For More Information

Books

Haldy, Emma E. *Helen Keller*. Ann Arbor, MI: Cherry Lake Publishing, 2017.

Kramer, Barbara. *Alexander Graham Bell*. Washington, DC: National Geographic Society, 2015.

Lambert, Joseph. *Annie Sullivan and the Trials of Helen Keller*. Los Angeles, CA: Disney Hyperion, 2018.

Websites

Alexander Graham Bell
www.ducksters.com/biography/alexander_graham_bell.php
Explore Bell's life on this website.

Fun Facts & Quotes About Helen Keller
braillebug.org/hkfacts.asp
Learn more about Keller through the Helen Keller Kids Museum.

Helen Keller
www.americaslibrary.gov/aa/keller/aa_keller_radcliffe_1.html
Learn more about Keller's road to college on this Library of Congress site.

INDEX